Better Than Yesterday

Dedication

This book is dedicated to my Mother and my

children and my Grandson thanks for always

motivating me to be a better version of myself

than I was yesterday I'm so grateful to God to be

your Daughter,Mother and Grandmother.

Table Of Contents

"Better Than Yesterday"

Introduction

As I thought about writing this book I

thought about how God brought me out of my

storms when I was on drugs, in 2012 and God

delivered me in 2015 even though I know I wasn't

out there bad it's bad whether or not people say

drugs are bad they are downers and I have

children and I love my children. My children are

depending on me, we are their role models as

parents. Each it's own being an addict is a

sickness but we get better when we do better.

Those of us that never been on drugs as well as

the ones that was and was delivered, shouldn't

think we're better than those on drugs, because

we are not. We all should help each other we

need each other's strength. I also thought about

this cps case I'm still on and and my children and

my smaller two are dismissed but they live with

my sister and brother in law and they are their

PMC which means permanent management

conservative. My two older children and their

Father got a chance to reunite through this case

and he said he was very sorry for not being

present in their lives and I forgave him. When we

get a second chance at being back in our

children's lives we have to watch out for satan

and his workers, so that we can really be involved

with our children because anything or "anyone"

else is irrelevant. If we really love our children

and want to get reunited and spend time with

them, we should do just that and don't let

"nothing" come between that. Im so grateful for

my sister and brother in law and I thank God for

them because they didn't have to help me and

my children, and they always want me to be

better in life. I'm glad I can see my children more,

and I'm involved in their lives but it hurts when

someone else has to raise your children and it's

your responsibility, but thank God for my

strength and my rights never was terminated

thanks be to God. Even though they let them be

their PMC I'm grateful for that because I was

living in hotels and every case in cps is different

from the next. It's a lot of people with "position

of power, or power position" that abuse their

power, and at the end of the day God sits high

and he looks low. At the time I got dismissed for

my smaller two children, I was living in hotels and

that was the only thing stopped me from getting

my children because I'm not on any drugs. My

daughter had to go out of state last year because

her behavior had to be stabilized I was told all

because of her past misbehaving but when

people are provoking a preteen and a teenager,

it's sad and it's your family but deep down I still

thank God for my family. I'm not justifying my

daughter's behavior when she did use to act up.

But when cps got her she was doing good living

with me and her grandmother before she went to

go live in Arkansas in her Center. When we have

the opportunity to help someone and we hurt

them instead God will punish you especially when

we mistreat children. CPS thought my daughter

didn't have a stable house because of what a

relative told them to see me hurt, but I forgive

and don't hold grudges, so that I can be better

than yesterday. When we are family we have to

really love each other and stop having favorites

and stop talking about your family when their

down because God do not like it, and he won't

bless us. We have to be careful and get our

blessings for our "good deeds" because God don't

blesses the "bad deeds." We have to remember

satan polishes up evil and make it look good, so

be careful and know the difference. I love and

miss my daughter very much and I never meant

to hurt my children and I'm very sorry for what I

put them through.

My daughter always say she's sorry for

running away from me to a stranger but as a

parent I shouldn't have scratched her trying to

keep her in the car after checking our flat tire

and I was drinking hours prior to what happened

and God knows I would never endanger my

children I love my children very much and would

never hurt my children, it was for my night job if

that night didn't happen to us. The Club was

BYOB that's why I bought the alcohol ahead of

time and I put it in my trunk that afternoon prior

to the incident to take to my night job where I

worked. I was honest to cps about drinking a

little alcohol that evening at a friends house. In

2022 last year, I don't know where a so call

positive hair follicle test came from because I do

not do any drugs. How can I be on drugs with a so

call positive hair follicle and a negative urine test

on the same day last year it's just sad, and God

knows that's wrong. In the beginning CPS should

have investigated the whole thing after knowing

that police hit my car from behind and he had my

daughter Eve in his car with him the whole time

when he hit us. I never wrecked my car, I had

the alcohol beverages in my trunk hours prior to that happening. I didn't leave my daughter intentionally I only left because I was sad and hurt that she wouldn't run back to me and her sister and brother and I went to get help. My daughter ran to a stranger to go get her charger from her grandmother's house. I didn't mean to hurt her and I'm very sorry for the hurt and pain I caused my daughter. Me and my daughter do have a good relationship, but she knows I'm the

mother regardless of what cps or others may

think. I was also on a previous case that a white

woman that used to live under me was rumored

to have slept with my man at the time called cps

and the police on me for nothing but not the stuff

we are in involved in now. I went to try and get

help after my daughter ran, when that lady kept

her in her car and wouldn't let her come back to

me. Most of the time, when we want to really be

of help to someone we should examine

everything before judging, because it's not what

it seem to be all the time. That Woman my

daughter ran too thought I was a bad parent and

once she saw the bruises she should have came

to me when I said I have other children in the car

with me.   We been involved in cps since July 31,

2020 and I pass all my test and everything. I

stayed in a hotel with my daughter Eve for nearly

a year and I don't know why they couldn't let my

smaller two children live with us. Nevertheless,

in 2021 I was told if you move in a hotel you

should get reunited with your children I don't see

why not it's considered a roof and you will have

food, but she still stated she wasn't promising

nothing because I still need a house. My daughter

was going to school from the hotel and I used to

live and work there. I just trust God and give it to

him and leave it there and he will reunite me and

my children. I was in a 9 year relationship with

my baby boy's father and it hurt but I had to let

him go or separate myself from him because he is

legally married and that's depriving me of getting

married, him and his wife never stayed in a house

together and they do not have children, but we

been through a lot and he always says he loves

me but straddling the fence is being a unstable

man and my children love him and he loves us

but he has to love himself. I know that he claims

he has been separated for a lot of years from her

before we ever started dating. One day I was

like, "he's not ever going to marry me." I now

know in order to be "better than yesterday, "we

have to let go of whatever and whoever holding

us down. You have to let go and let God remove

whatever or whoever is weighing you down. You

don't need that thing or that person you pray to

God about because what he's telling you, is to let

go of it, so that he can have your full undivided

attention; so that he can bless you.

Now I look back it was my actions that

caused the entire thing and the police or that lady

would never thought I was a bad parent and that

still don't give a Officer a right to beat on a

civilian. Better than yesterday means we are

living for today and the future and whatever is in

the past needs to stay there and whoever hurt

you, you have to forgive them for yourself and

move on. We will become better than yesterday

once we realize it's ok if you failed at something

just don't stay there and deep down I'm grateful

for CPS regardless of what we may think of them

and I know that I'm a good parent but we all need

direction and guidance and God always puts

people in our path to help us, and it don't mean

that we are bad parents. When this case first

happened I felt ashamed and couldn't believe

that this was happening to my family, but I gave it

to God and I casted it to him.

Only God can heal us and deliver us, and he

has his way of doing just that and it's his timing

and he will see us through whatever it is just trust

him and stay prayed up in your trails and

tribulations and know that trouble don't last

always. Weeping may endure through the night,

but joy comes in the morning. If any of you is

going through a CPS case, or if you are going

through something in order to become better

than yesterday, you have to trust the process do

what you have to do and don't let your children

down. Our circumstances don't make us who we

are, it's what we do in our circumstances, that

mean we will make it through. We will be alright

and things will get better we have to know that

things will get better and want better and do

better and we will be better than yesterday, and

when we have challenges we will know how to

deal with them. Being better than yesterday

takes time, time is our friend and rushing is not

good and taking your time on working on you

takes time, when you becoming a better version

of yourself than yesterday.

Chapter 1.

"Good Things Come To Those Who"

My Mother always says, "good things come to those who wait." Every time someone hurt me she always comfort me with that and it makes feel better whenever I'm going through something or when I want better because things takes time. Whatever is in the past is in the past and we have to move on, and pray and forgive those that hurt us and don't dwell

on it. When we hold grudges if we hurt

somebody vice versa and claiming we are

better we are only fooling ourselves. When

somebody don't accept our apology we have

to remember the serenity prayer because, "we

have to accept the things we can not change."

We have to want better and do better and

what's in the past is done and it's over, it's a

new day because yesterday is behind us.

Don't cry over spilled milk, what is gone

is gone and be a better you than yesterday.

Whatever is meant will be but life must go on.

Bad things do happen to good people. But we

have to take the bitter with the sweet and

move on. Life is like a movie, it's different

scenes that brings us to the next, for instance

like foreshadowing we are going to think

about past things and we are going to have

some flashbacks. We have to get to the next

day or next scene to make it to the next, so

that we can get a award at the end and in life.

At the end of every rainy day it's a beautiful

rainbow, so be ready, so that God will say;

"we'll done my good and faithful servant."

We can not dwell on the past and make a

better future it's only going to effect our

future. Whoever hurt me or did me wrong I

know how to forgive and move on because

holding grudges is only going to make matters

worse and delay our blessings. When we

forgive we have to know it's not for the other

person when we forgive them because

forgiveness is for us not for the other person.

To be better than yesterday we have to stay

humble no matter what when we don't have

money like we used to have or if we don't

have that dream job or that Husband or Wife

don't beat yourself it will come to pass we

have to walk by faith and not by sight and God

will bless you, and his timing is better than

ours and his thoughts are far away from us.

If you did all that you could in a

relationship, and it's toxic don't think you are

the problem and kept going back and it still

don't work out it's not you because you are

not the problem that person don't know what

love is. A toxic relationship will drain you that

isn't love, and it's not healthy, real love is felt

when both people really love each other and

want the best for one another. God will bless

you, you have to trust God and he will deliver

you from whatever you are going through. We

have to remember we can't change people but

we can change our situation, pray for them

and ourselves and change for the better to

make our lives better. Just because a

relationship doesn't work out or you may be at

a job that you really don't want to be at, that

don't mean you not going to get that dream

job. We have to keep pushing towards our

mark for greatness until we get to where God

wants us to be and thank him for where we

are right then, so that we will get there.

Complaining only delay our blessing when we

have a on time God, so remember that is who

we are pleasing and who gives us our

approval.

God never makes mistakes, but we do

because we are only human. "Life is what we

make it, so make the best of it why we can

because there are no excuses, no matter your

age and failure is not an option." We have to

know that we gave it our all in relationships

that didn't work out, or jobs that really didn't

see our potential or see just our failures,

because failure only makes future Athletes,

Doctors, Lawyers, Policemen and Policewomen

and Musicians, Rappers etc etc or what you

want to be, you can accomplish it just stay

committed and consistent you will achieve it.

In order to be the best you have to work at

bring the best. In being the best most think

that mean no messing up or failing. In school

when a Teacher give a student a test at first if

you fail, you study and study and studying

makes you pass the test the next time. So

failure do not mean stay where you are, it

precisely means to go after something if you

want to be the best or get that good grade

after a failing one and it's the same in life, just

because you get lemons doesn't means it's

sour just make lemonade. Failure do not mean

it's the end, it's the end if you want it to be,

please don't give up because giving up

shouldn't never be in your success goals if you

want to be successful.

Doubting will not get you where you

need to be to accomplish your goals or Dreams

you have to stick with it and keep going to be

better than yesterday because we are going to

fail, but just don't stay there. Our dreams

comes true when we make goals, write them

down, and visualize them. We have to do

what we set out to do, we can't just think

about them and let years go by, and get to

comfortable because we want accomplish

nothing. We can take breaks but just don't

take long ones when you want to be successful

at something or reaching your dreams or

pursuing them. We can't listen to people that's

not going where God is going to take us

because they care nothing about seeing us

become better than yesterday if they don't see

themselves being better than yesterday.

Our character has a lot to do with us

being better, if we want to be better, then we

must do better. It's going to be a lot of

obstacles in the way, life is like a roller coaster,

it's goes up and it's goes down but it do stop

just long as you don't give up in life. Life is like

a movie, you should do what you going to do if

you want to be a villain, or the protagonist and

the antagonist it's up to you the villain

sometimes dies in the movie or go to jail or

something bad happens to him for hurting

people or doing people wrong etc etc. No

matter what happens in our lives we must

separate ourselves from people that is not

adding value to our lives and no the difference

between good friends or bad friends because

that has a lot to with being a better you. It's

good to make friends but it's important to stay

in good company, because bad company

corrupts good character.

Chapter 2.

"Forgive Them For Yourself"

I remember when I was a teenager, a in-

law came between me and my Family he took

advantage of me sexually and I was only

sixteen years old about to turn seventeen and

it was embarrassing and I had to call the police

on him and I went to the hospital and I got

examined and the proof was right there and

my relative still didn't believe her children's

father sexually molested me or sexually

abused me. First of all it was so shameful back

then. I was so hurt and that relative and I was

really close growing up, it hurt me that she

didn't believe me and ever since I was a little

girl I love everything about her. She is very

strong and I still admire her tenacity and how

she don't let nothing bother her. I'm just glad

today that I can talk about what happened to

me when I was sixteen and I didn't in my first

book because a person I love and respect that

raised me said, "please don't talk about what

happen to you when you was a teenager

because she showing you how much she loves

you and your children. When a person really

love you and helping you they shouldn't hold

grudges, in being better than yesterday

because it's going to delay your blessings

that's coming for the next day and thereafter.

We hurt ourselves waiting on people to

change we have to pray for them. We really

could be good people, but having a bad

attitude and doing things out of spite to hurt

somebody makes you a bad person. It's my

blood sweat and tears and my book, and

children, teenagers and people in general are

going through things and need help. I don't

throw my family to the wolves because I love

them and it's all out of love and being better

than yesterday and letting things go that's

been weighing us down.

I'm ver grateful for a support system and

even though people may not support you the

way you support them doesn't mean they are

not supporting you. When people get a

position of power we have to be careful when

God bless us to help others, and do not hurt

and help at the same time because God is a

jealous God.

I'm very grateful for a support them to

doesn't mean they power we have to be

careful when God blesses us to help others. I

felt as though I had to talk about this in this

book because that has something to do with

being better than yesterday. Everything and

everyone is not all what it looks like. If any of

you experiencing or experienced sexually

abuse from a in law, or relative or sexually

abuse in general, you are not alone. If you let

them do it and you was scared or if it was

force and if you was a child, or a teenager

don't feel bad if nobody don't believe you

because God sees all and knows all. We have

to forgive people for ourselves and move on

we don't know why things happens the way

they do, and when people talks to certain

people in the family and they treat you as if

you the one that came between the family,

don't worry about it just pray and stay

focused. If you was a child or a teenager and

people that hurt you don't care about what

they did and hurt you and their own family all

you can do is keep praying for them and

yourself and forgive who hurt you. We all have

to forgive them for ourselves so that we can

move on, because the hurt and damages is

done vice versa it's too late but we can be

better than yesterday and stop holding

grudges and love your family. Life is not

promised and death is an old friend we have

to be careful how we treat others because God

want us to love and help each other. Most

families have darker secrets that people think

is normal but its dysfunctional. If you are

going through something you are not alone

just stay prayed up it hurts when someone

forces themselves on you and you are all alone

and scared and you know they saw you grow

up and you don't know why this person is on

top of you and you know it's wrong. Even if

you didn't fight them back you are still the

victim and if you called the police and you still

get blamed just give it to God, and tell

someone like I did. If you can't talk to your

family, and if you are in school stay focused on

your studies and God. Before and Afterward I

know that it hurt I was just like you, you trust

somebody and they take advantage of you and

then your family think you the bad guy. If you

have problems in your family and once you are

a grown up and you notice things are not like it

once was when you were a kid just pray. You

and your family can have meetings or make up

a family group chat like my family and talk

things out but not talk about each other on

there, if you are a close family stay that way.

You can have dinners and enjoy one another

or talk to a relative that you can trust about

whatever it is because you need your family. If

your family, a co worker, a friend, etc etc hurt

you so bad just distance yourself and pray and

tell God to help you because he knows you

want everyone and including yourself to be

better but we can't save everyone.   We can

only pray for them, once you see they like

gossiping and doing evil deeds just stay away

from them. To be better than yesterday you

have to figure out the solutions after knowing

the problem, in order to move forward so that

it won't hinder you on your journey. If the

other person don't want to be better than

yesterday they have to want it own their own

we can't force change but we can start with us

so that you won't bring the past hurt and pain

in your future. I remember when I was a

teenager I had a lot of money and I helped a

lot of family out that needed me. Now that I

need help with somewhere to stay and I don't

have the amount of taxes this year because I

didn't carry my smaller children it's taking a

little time to get a place for me and my

children on cps. I remember my Pastor Joel

Osteen saying, "they might not help you the

way you help them or applaud you for your

accomplishments and if they do don't be mean

like them just because their ugly towards you

just give it to God, because you can't change

people minds and opinions of you but you can

pray for them." We have to forgive and move

on and when God elevate us to our destiny or

when that breakthrough and blessing comes

that you been praying for you stay the same

and humble because God is going to bless you

just don't give up. Love conquers all things

when all else fail you. I love when Pastor

Osteen say, "Stop looking at how big the

problem is and look at how big and powerful

your God is." God will not put no more on us

than we can bare. When somebody do us

wrong or mistreat us and they claim they are

helping you and doing you a favor and they are

being ugly to you, and they end up on the

other side of the fence help them and don't be

mad or hold grudges like they done you and let

God be the glory. Remember God when your

breakthrough comes and do what you told

God you will do and always give him thanks

because he created us and everything we have

comes from him. I remember in 2014, some

family member called cps on me and my

children and I had to go live with my oldest

sister. While I was pregnant my relative beat

on me pregnant with my daughter Genesis and

the doctor said if I have stayed there while

getting beaten any longer My daughter and I

could have died. The only thing that I didn't

understand was I was on cps and they didn't

even investigate it but wanted a urinalysis test

just sad and I had a unborn in my stomach that

almost died, and they represent Children and

never asked was me and the baby ok. Every

time I see that relative he always say how

sorry he is and I always tell him I forgive you

and he just like my little brother and I love him

very much since he was a baby and I know

satan had him because he was lost back then.

Satan comes has a wolve in sheep's clothing

we have to be careful who we think love us

and want our best interest. We have to

Forgive those that persecute us and let God

handle the evil deeds they are doing and you

just keep thriving and stay focus, and

remember forgive them for yourself so that

you can be better.

Chapter 3.

"You Can Love You Better"

When the hurt is over after being in a

toxic relationship don't rush into a new one

right away. You are powerful and believe and

know that, just because you are bitter doesn't

mean you want get better. Having a wrong

mindset about a person are thing will keep you

doubting and missing your blessing and delay

them. Just because someone hurt you that

don't mean stay mad and frustrated at the

person, but just think power thoughts and see

yourself as a powerful person like God sees

you that's how you activate powerful thinking.

Thinking of yourself as a loser, or saying, "I'm

not going to find someone like him or her and I

been with them too long I don't want to start

over," will keep you being with the wrong

person for the wrong reason and in the end

you still not happy. You can love you better

you just have to see yourself as being

whatever God says you are. It don't cost you

nothing to love you, and loving yourself is the

best thing that you can do especially when you

find yourself by yourself. Ultimately you

suppose to love yourself when you in a

relationship, marriage, or friendship so that if

it don't work out you still have you. Self care

or self preservation is close to God, then and

only then you can help the next person.

Loving yourself starts with proper eating

habits, taking vitamins, taking good baths,

spiritual healing baths at times with candles

and soft music. You have to get plenty of rest

so that you will be productive in life. You can't

keep partying and saying you want better. In

the Bible the Apostle Paul said, "when I

became a man I put childish things behind

me." We can't keep doing what we did at 15

and expect to be better than yesterday. Make

a to do list of things to do or get you a planner

that help as well, and keep up with your

appointments and start keeping things in

order that you didn't do before. Grocery

shopping is good if you don't always do the

shopping , it keeps your mind occupied. Treat

yourself to a dinner, or a movie, if you have

children go to the park like me and my

children do I love seeing my children play it's

fun and that's exercise as well. Loving you is

the most important thing you can do, because

it's no one's duty to love you but you, and

"you can love you better." Break ups are hard,

no one wants to just go through them to be

going through them, especially when you

really love someone and you thought they

loved you. Break ups can be your new

beginning to a better you, and getting a better

person than you previously had. Breaking up

with someone most of the time is God's way of

warning you about someone or something, but

not all break ups are bad. Most people know

how to let go of people, and then you have

those that just don't know how to let others

go because it's hard for them. We have to be

careful about what kind of person we want to

date especially if you have children like I do

because I love my children. Our blessings will

be delayed if we are doing the wrong thing

and hurting the ones that love us and don't

worry about what they did to you.   Just

because a person has a position of power or

power position doesn't mean they can't get

found out on and brought down because God

know what they are doing is wrong and he

blessed them and they are leading people

astray. If you have a parent or friends etc etc

that treats other children better than you and

they get together and talk about you just stay

prayed up and remember your intentions and

stay humble, and don't worry about theirs

because God will make your enemies your

footstool. God will punish them for what they

done to you and especially if you helped them

at their lowest and they take advantage of you

at yours. If you really been a good kid and you

do all you can for your parent and they are

toxic and always saying God is going to punish

you just let them talk, and you just keep being

a good child and keep honoring your parents

it's a blessing with your name on it. God sees

and looks at the heart and he's our Judge. I

know you may have been heartbroken by a

man or woman and they look at you for

everything and most people may think they

really love you and take care of you, and you

may be shame to divorce them or break up

with them. I know that you may been the

couple that everyone admires, but when you

are not happy, you just not happy and staying

in a toxic relationship is not healthy. I been

there, you have to be the bigger person and

end the relationship, especially if you have

children. You are your children's role models

and God gave you the responsibility as their

Parent to guide, instruct, disciplined and have

them to grow up the way that God wants them

to be.

Chapter 4.

"I Found Love Without Going No Where"

You have to love you right where you are,

because the truth of the matter is you can go

looking it for love in all the wrong places, but

you first have to love yourself. We can't love

no one else until we love ourselves. We can't

have a diseased heart and expect to get healed

and truly blessed. I was in a 9 year

relationship with who I thought was the love

of my life, I love everything about this man

and we have a smart, handsome and funny 6

year old son together that wants to be a police

when he grows up. I waited patiently for him

to divorce his wife in which they were

separated he claimed when we first started

talking. I never understood why he would

stay married close to 30 years to her and they

never stayed together in a house and she's on

drugs living in a crack house and they don't

have children together supposedly. Time after

time he claimed he would divorce her and he

claims she don't want to sign papers etc etc

but I know now, that this man is in love with

that woman. It hurt because we were in a long

term relationship and he never loved me like I

loved him but I know how to let go, because

somebody has to. I felt so stupid over the

years knowing he love her and living in my

house and one day God spoke to me he said, "I

know he is married and he don't want her

anymore he loves you but I'm not pleased with

him leading you astray." Love is blind and I do

believe that because I was the kind of person

saying I will never be with a married man, or

will not be with a man I don't know. In fact

we have history together through our son and

he's been in my family before I was ever born.

He said they were separated and I should have

never talked to him in the first place knowing

he was married.

Ladies and men when someone uses that phrase while dating run because most of the time they are still involved with him or her, so be careful and choose wisely. Love never hurts, never fail or doubts, and you will know when the right man or woman comes you just have to be working on you before they arrive because you don't have to go anywhere love will eventually find you! For the last five months I been talking long distance to a man

that I fell in love with through my cousin he

saw me on some pictures of his and he wanted

to get to know me so one day he called me

from another country and we been

communicating for months now and we

decided to make it official a few months ago.

I'm in love with him he's 29 and I'm in my 40's

and he is man enough for me. I introduce him

to my Mother and my children and the rest of

my family and they like him. I'm very grateful

for my new love and thank God for him

everyday, because he's everything I always

wanted and love me and I love him. I never

thought I would find someone that truly love

me I thought it was my previous boyfriend but

he just want to stay married and have his cake

and eat it and think I have to accept it. I

allowed myself to be victimized in a toxic

relationship that wasn't never ever going

anywhere, but one day I said I know he's a

good man to me and my children and we love

him, then I said I have to leave him so that I

can really be happy. I had the right mindset

before I met my new love that makes me feels

so good, and his words and how he talks to me

soothe my soul. I never meant to hurt my little

boy's father while he was in jail, because my

mind was made up long before I ever met my

new found love. I still help him from time to

time, if he need anything because I believe you

don't kick a person when their down. I know

my ex never had a woman to love him the way

I did because I showed him I did. I hope he

move on like I did and don't hold grudges and

really know I was in love with him but I want

better for me and my children. Regardless of

what's in black and white it's about my

children and we can't make somebody stay

married or get a divorce and children didn't

ask to come here. We can't make children and

pretend they don't exist because God knows

and what's done in the dark will eventually

come to the light. We may think we are getting

away with something but we have to answer

to God and don't get mad when the ones we

hurt and mistreated no longer wants us.

Children don't stay children forever and we

must love them and not abandon or disown

them and take care of our responsibility, and

they don't forget when they grow up. Its our

responsibility to raise them the way that God

told us in his word, and when all else fail us,

we can't let them down. He was a good man,

father, and father figure to my children. I'm

getting older and I don't want to waste my life

with the wrong person and never really be

happy.

I want to be married like my sisters and I

can't keep allowing myself to think I'm in love

and I'm not. I know God has so much for me

and my children and wants me to accomplish a

lot of things in life and he wants me to do

great things.

My Pastor Joel says, "you can't be

thinking weak if you are a strong powerful

person." In order to get what God has for you

you have to let go of some things and some

people because they can't go where God is

about to take you. I know God don't want me

with a married man, and I know a lot of you

may be in relationships just like I was it's

dangerous when you really don't know if the

person going to marry you and wasting your

time and they think you stupid. That old

saying is true and it's a song also that says, "I

been looking for love in all the wrong places,"

and this time I fell in love and I didn't have to

go no where. Love will find you, if you are

looking for it or not it's God's timing not ours,

and just let God guide you and I'm not bitter

anymore I'm blessed. Being unhappy is not a

good feeling, you have to put on a smile and

act as if you really happy when in fact you not

and that's also unhealthy. Trust God and he

will guide you he knows what we need before

we even ask him, and God will make our

cricket places straight. I remember Pastor

Osteen, saying, "we can't make people love us

or treat us right, but the change we want to

see starts with us." Yes they hurt you and God

will turn it around for your good. Don't bring

people that don't mean you no good to where

God is about to take you, because everybody

can't go to where God is about to take you, so

stop trying to bring them. I love when my

Pastor says, "God will take you places you

never dreamed of or imagined and see

yourself the way God sees you." Yes they said

ugly hateful things about you and said you will

never be nothing, but keep a good mindset

and think powerful thoughts about yourself.

Love never fails it will find you just because

you went through a few bad apples the tree

still have good ones. I see people as trees if it's

fruitful, it's a good person, if it's a lot of rotten

apples they are bad and you can tell a tree by

its roots meaning, you will know if a person

has good or bad intensions. Don't let what

they did to you, stop you your blessings

because God is about to bless you for being

humble, meek and steadfast and for

persevering through it all and for keeping him

in the midst.

Chapter 5.

"You Can't Get Better Until You Do Better"

It's a old saying that goes like this, if you

want better you have to do better, and "you

can't get better until you do better." Whatever

you set out to do in life you can not doubt you

have to trust God and yourself, but if you are

doubting that's what's stopping your blessing

from coming any sooner or they will be

delayed. A unstable person is unstable in all

their ways. Knowing who you are and what

you want to do in life is important, not giving

up and believing in yourself, is the key to

happiness and success. In school when a

student takes notes opposed to a student that

don't like writing notes will make a better

grade or be successful at any test. Being ready

and prepared in life shows he or she is

equipped and willing while the teacher is

teaching and that's what life is about and

following your dreams and doing something

about them. You can say all day you want to

be something, but if you are not doing nothing

about it you will not get to where you are

going because you just talking about it. You

have to walk and talk and keep going in life.

Just because you might fail at something

doesn't mean you are not good at it. You have

to keep at it until you get better and that is

what life is all about.

When you give up, you don't know what could

have been, but when you keep going you have

a chance at something great and being great at

whatever it is because you didn't quit. Quitters

never win and winners never quit, and

eloquently that's the beauty of it. Staying in

the game is what all players want, but all the

best players stay in the game and the ones on

the side is waiting to get in the game so they

can show what they can do to. When you get

that opportunity at whatever it may be, be

good at it and that may be your last

opportunity at it and don't let no one stop

you. You can't get better until you do better.

Better just want come overnight you have to

separate yourself in a category of losers and

winners, because misery loves company.   You

was chosen for such a time like this to be that

person in your family that's going all the way

and you not letting no one stop you as you

make that dream come true to change your

situation and your living conditions to have

better for you and your family. Remember

giving up is easy nothing comes in giving up, so

go all way and persevere and get your

blessings, because better can't come until you

do better. Better will come long as you willing

and staying focused no matter what it is stay

humble God will give it to you. Trouble don't

last always and better days are coming, just

believe when God says he will bless you for

being mistreated, abused made fun of for

doing the right things. Keep thriving for

greatness and see yourself as a giant to small

minded people. David was a Shepherd boy

that believe God will deliver him and his

people from Goliath and that's what we have

to do with our faith and with what we have

and know that we can make giants fall too.

Don't be scared of bullies, they only want

attention and will run over you if you do not

stand up to them.

If you are experiencing a bully tormenting you

whether or not you are in school, college or at

work etc etc because deep down they are

scared people. Bullies just need to be told no

and just let them know you demand respect

you don't have to fight are be violent just

show them you not scared and do what God

did for David and you will defeat any giant or

bully. I remember kids used to bully me in

elementary at E.J Scott Elementary School and

my cousins and friends used to go tell my

brother Jody and afterwards at home he

would ask me is this boy bullying you at school

Felicia, and I would lie to my brother because

my brother knows how to fight and he was not

scared of bullies growing up. One day my

brother came up to my school waited after

school and asked the bully did he knew Felicia

Martin and why did he say yes, and he said,

"yes I beat her freaking but up everyday." My

brother beat him up and blacked his eyes and

busted and his lips. I was sad he did it but just

like that bullies are scared little people deep

down. I'm not saying it's cool to bully people

or go beat up someone, I'm just sharing my

story as a kid to help whoever reads better than yesterday, and hopefully it helps you. I loved the story in Dr. JPrince book "Respect," because he talks about how he beat up the school bullying at Dogan Elementary and he was short and the bully was very tall and after that he got mush respect. I love how my Pastor tells a story of a little boy and his father and the little boy's father bought him a telescope. The little boy was looking in it one

day backwards at a bully, and his father asked

him why he had it that way he said I like it like

this because it makes the bully looks small. We

have to see our problems, bills, bad friends, or

toxic relationships, bullies etc etc as small as

well because God don't want you around

those kinds of people or he don't want you

worry about things because he is a powerful

God.

Chapter 6.

"Think It, Write It, Vision It, Make It Happen

It's always important to think about what

you want do in life then write your goals,

accomplishments, achievements and dreams

down on paper; then vision it then make it

happen. If you can think it you can can see

yourself doing whatever it is then put action

with what you set out to do and then that will

be your dreams coming true when you do

something about making them come true. It's

good to always make a to do list, whether or

not it's a simple grocery list and check off what

you placed in the basket so that way you want

be working backwards and that's what the

title of this chapter is about because if you

never think about your goals you will never

write them down or vision them or do

something about them, so that you can be

successful to change your living conditions.

Only you can change your living conditions not

your Mother, not your Father or your siblings

or friends, it depends on you, and it starts and

ends with you. You can see all the famous

people in the world and wonder how they got

there it's hard work, dedication and doing

things you never done before. To get

something you never had you have to do

something you never did before to be

successful or famous if that's what you want,

and don't let anyone talk you out of it because

that's what's going to help you and your family

to have better lives. Once you have the right

mindset and see yourself how God sees you

then that's when you activate thinking

powerful thoughts in becoming all that God

wants you to be. You have to see yourself as a

Giant like David he told Goliath I'm not alone

and he told him he would defeat him and

that's what we have to do when we're facing

something or someone. Always know that

God is with you when you think you are alone

he's carrying you like the parable in the Bible,

that's is when God carrying you when you

think he's not.

We should see ourselves as giants and

don't be scared to face them and make them

tremble and knock them down and win. The

moral of the story of David is he used what he

had which was a sling shot and first of all his

faith and just like David God is with us as well

and he's equipped us with the tools and we

are powerful as well. No matter if we are a

Mother, just don't say, "I'm just a mother how

can God use me," because just like Deborah in

the Bible he used her to better her entire city

and community through a Mother and her

faith. So stop saying, " I'm a mother God can't

use me I'm not like the people in the Bible," of

course you are they were people just like you

and me and they did it and so can we. We

don't have to go anywhere blessings comes to

us, love will find you right where you are but

be ready when it comes and don't be saying

are you sure you want me etc etc and stop

making excuses you are powerful and God

created you to do great things. God wants to

bless you from a victim and be a victor or from

a Victoria to be victorious, so get the victory

he wants to give you. I remember when I was

14 years old, after our big brother Pete was

murdered, I asked my brother Jody to write

me a rap. I thought about music as I was day

dreaming one day and I asked him to wrote

me a rap. When I asked my brother to write

me a rap it looked like he wanted to say why,

but he didn't, as he was writing the rap I saw

myself as a rapper on stage and thereafter I

always wrote my own raps. years after my

brother wrote my first rap I wrote" Jobs

Faith," in 2007 and self published it in 2021

and this book your reading now is my second

book thanks be to God we have to "think it,

write it, vision it, and then make it happen and

it will come to pass.

God said it in his word he will bless you

because of your faith and because you are

righteous and because you doing it in

remembrance of him, for the better of

mankind and not for self gain. God will bless

you with your talents and gifts, but you have

to be taking notes, making goals write them

down and see yourself doing it and be working

until he blesses you and stay focused and keep

going and help others after he bless you and

that's how you make God smile. I remember

my previous pastor saying, "it's enough

people in the cemetery and in prison that have

dreams and goals they never pursued or

accomplished. Don't be a person that put off

what you should be doing today for tomorrow,

because tomorrow is not promised. We have

to be better and in becoming "better than

yesterday it takes time and if it's an addiction

or whatever it may be, don't give up it takes

time and stay prayed up and you will be

better in life. We all have a race in life, so

don't rush and don't waste it doing nothing be

working and praying and helping others until

the end and be working and you will win your

own race.

"Conclusion"

You Can't be "better than yesterday",until you

want better and not living in the past and if

you want a better today it means letting go of

things that's irrelevant towards being your

best today because "yesterday" is gone a

better future lies ahead if you are committed

and consistent, my late Father taught me it's

not about how we start but precisely about

how we finish. I live when my mother says, "a

race horse runs fast but not long," so don't be

a person that's running and not going no

where. We have to let the hurt go, the shame,

the addictions, and afflictions as well no one

is better than the next we need each other's

strengths. Remember my strengths may not be

yours or vice versa, but when we come

together we are better like that than

separated. Also remember to see real change

starts with being "better than yesterday after

God blessed us to see today in order to get to

a brighter future.

All the scriptures I said in "Better Than

Yesterday," are in my own words, and is kept

in context and they are from the "Holy Bible"

and "New International Version."

About The Author

Felicia Denise Martin is from

Houston,Texas she is a new self published

Author she has four children, two sons and

two daughters and a grandson. Felicia loves

her children and grandson and her Family and

she loves spending time with her children and

her family. Felicia loves cooking, reading,

writing, swimming, shooting pool and enjoy

having picnics with her children and she loves

writing books and she loves helping her

community and she wants to touch all people

with her books and she loves people, and

"Better Than Yesterday" is her second book

thus far and she has plans to write plenty

more books. She believes to be "better than

yesterday" we must let the past go and be

committed to change and stay consistent in

seeing it in ourselves, in order to grow and to

be better starts with bettering ourselves

before we can help others.

Ms. Felicia Author's link is

www.Amazon.com/author/felicia